The
White House
Easter Egg Roll

Text by
C. L. Arbelbide

Illustrations by
Barbara Leonard Gibson

Published by
White House Historical Association
Washington, D.C.

The WHITE HOUSE HISTORICAL ASSOCIATION
is a non-profit organization, chartered on November 3, 1961,
to enhance understanding, appreciation, and enjoyment of the Executive
Mansion. The Association's headquarters is located at 740 Jackson
Place, NW, Washington, DC, 20503-0300.

Copyright © 1997 White House Historical Association
Library of Congress Number 97-60317
ISBN 0-912308-70-2

Staff for this book: Donald J. Crump, Editorial Director;
Susan A. Franques, Researcher; Martha C. Christian, Contributing Editor.

The staff wishes to thank the following
individuals for their assistance on this project: Garrett W.
Arbelbide, Caitlin Mary Kiss, Donald R. Kennon, Louis B. Raffel, Cecilia
Glembocki, Eileen Jinks, Philip L. Maynard, Joseph Biebel, Steve Ison, Henry
Haller, D. Michael Ressler, Christine A. Kohn. White House Staff: Rex W.
Scouten, William G. Allman, Lydia Barker Tederick, Irvin M. Williams,
Betty C. Monkman, John A. Moeller, Joni Stevens, and Robyn Dickey.

Contributing organizations include:
The National Park Service, "The President's Own" Marine Band,
American Egg Board, Virginia Egg Council, The Library of Congress,
Martin Luther King Library, Arlington (Virginia) Central Library, U.S. Capitol
Historical Society, Franklin D. Roosevelt Library, Harry S. Truman Library,
Ronald Reagan Library, Rutherford B. Hayes Library, Herbert C. Hoover
Library, Richard M. Nixon Presidential Project (National Archives),
John Fitzgerald Kennedy Library, Lyndon Baines Johnson Library,
George W. Bush Library, Gerald R. Ford Library, Jimmy
Carter Library, and Dwight D. Eisenhower Library.

Printed by Southeastern Color Graphics, Inc.,
Johnson City, TN; color separations by CMI Color Graphix, Inc.,
Huntingdon Valley, PA; binding by Quebecor, Kingsport, TN; typesetting
by CompuPrint Of Washington, Inc., Washington, DC.

THE WHITE HOUSE
Washington, D.C.

Dear Reader,

President Clinton and I always enjoy that special day each year when thousands of smiling children join us in the nation's backyard for the White House Easter Egg Roll.

This colorful festival, created by children, found its way to the White House in 1878, and is one of the oldest traditions of this grand old home of Presidents.

The President, Chelsea, and I invite you to come be our guest at the next Easter Egg Roll, share the fun, and be a part of White House history.

Hillary Rodham Clinton

It's Monday after Easter; it's egg-rolling day,
And the White House invites you to join in the play.

No matter who is President, each and every year,
Egg-rolling day is full of fun and good cheer.

Here is the story of how it all came to be,
A very special day in White House history.

A long time ago, on a school holiday,
Capitol Hill was a great place to play.

Rolling colorful eggs down the grassy hill,
Tumbling close behind just like Jack and Jill!

Inside the Capitol, beneath the big dome,
Children ate lunch, feeling right at home.

Many of the Congressmen didn't like this at all.
Picnic mess and eggshells cluttered their great hall!

Then one Easter Monday, policemen said, "No.
A new law says, you must take your eggs and go."

No picnics allowed; no one can pass.
All egg-rollers must "Keep off the grass!"

President and Mrs. Hayes would save the day,
Inviting the children to the White House to play.

The President's backyard was the perfect place,
Hills for egg-rolling and plenty of space.

Room to jump rope, and picnic under trees,
Room to trade eggs and Easter memories.

John Philip Sousa stood on a stand,
Directing the music of the Marine Band.

Their red coats were brilliant; their instruments shone,
Every trumpet and flute and golden trombone.

Hand-clapping, toe-tapping, music fast and slow,
People laughing, children dancing — moving to and fro.

To meet President Harrison, children everywhere,
Squeezed into the East Room, not an inch to spare.

Their giggles and laughter added to the fun.
A loose balloon floated past George Washington.

Children at the fountain, sailing egg-shell boats,
Talking, laughing, asking, "Would they stay afloat?"

As they bobbed and bobbed, more children came,
To sail their tiny boats and join in this new game.

Waiting, waiting, waiting — children wanting to go in,
Standing, standing, standing — when, when, when?

Thank goodness for the vendor who lingered on the street,
Selling to egg-rollers their favorite ice cream treat.

Finally, finally, finally, the line began to budge,
Slowly, slowly, slowly — nudge, nudge, nudge.

The line is getting shorter; we'll be inside soon.
Wait — I'll be right back — I want a red balloon!

Even the White House pets came to play,
Joining the fun on egg-rolling day.

Dashing about, bringing laughter and joy,
Was President Harding's dog, Laddie Boy.

From his favorite spot, the wicker stand,
Performing tricks and shaking hands.

Grace Coolidge had many stories to tell,
About Rebecca Raccoon, her animal pal.

A furry ringed tail and a mask she wore.
Few children had seen a raccoon before.

Look! A chocolate bunny standing five feet tall,
Lady Bird Johnson's gift, shared by one and all.

The next year Pat Nixon brought a special guest,
A giant Easter Bunny, and children were impressed.

Ever since that visit, each and every year,
The White House Easter Bunny on this day appears.

Chefs in tall white hats prepare for egg-rolling play,
They have to boil and color thousands of eggs today.

Boiling and boiling — steam rises in the air,
Coloring and drying — hard-boiled eggs everywhere.

Using every basket, every pan, every pot,
Filling the White House kitchen with colored polka dots!

Children, side by side, color and create,
Taking turns to draw and to decorate.

Yellow eggs, green eggs, colored eggs galore,
Flowered eggs, striped eggs, all of this and more.

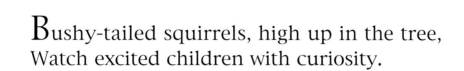

Bushy-tailed squirrels, high up in the tree,
Watch excited children with curiosity.

Hide-and-seek, hide-and-seek — eggs in the hay,
"I found one, I found one, to take home today!"

Egg-rolling day was ending? Kids could not believe.
Hadn't it just started? Now it's time to leave?

Did they have a good time? Egg-rollers gave their reply,
"Let's do this every day, except Christmas and the Fourth of July."

Then, shouting in voices heard loud and clear,
"Thank you, Mr. and Mrs. President! We'll be back next year!"

History of the White House Easter Egg Roll

Informal egg-rolling parties were hosted at the White House by President Andrew Johnson and, in 1873 by President Grant. But, the liveliest of these events in the 1870s took place at the U.S. Capitol.

1876:   Senate Bill No. 700 is introduced April 19. Bill passed April 29 to keep egg rolling off the Capitol grounds.

1878:   Federal law enforced April 22. President and Mrs. Hayes offer their backyard, giving egg rolling an "official" home.

1889:   President Benjamin Harrison requests "The President's Own," Marine Band to play, with John Philip Sousa directing.

1917:   Canceled because of World War I. Children roll their eggs at the Capitol and the National Zoo. President and Mrs. Harding resume the White House party in 1921.

1929:   Lou Hoover introduces maypole and folk dancing activities.

1942:   Canceled because of World War II. As Easter of 1946 nears, President Truman encourages "the conservation of food," and cancels the egg roll. President and Mrs. Eisenhower revive the event in 1953.

1974:   Pat Nixon organizes egg-rolling races, and adds spoons from the White House kitchen.

1975:   Betty Ford introduces Ukrainian egg-decorating demonstrations. Plastic eggs are used in egg roll. Real eggs return in 1977.

1980:   Rosalynn Carter gives out 10,000 souvenir plastic eggs with a welcome message inside.

1981:   Nancy Reagan, who attended the egg roll as a child, introduces the egg hunt and autographed souvenir wooden eggs.

1991:   Barbara Bush provides special Easter cards to be mailed to the troops in the Persian Gulf in Operation Desert Storm.

1993:   Hillary Rodham Clinton expands the egg roll to the Ellipse to include additional activities for both children and adults.